RACIAL JUSTICE IN AMERICA
HISTORIES

TULSA RACE RIOTS and the RED SUMMER of 1919

KEVIN P. WINN WITH KELISA WING

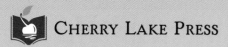
CHERRY LAKE PRESS

Published in the United States of America by Cherry Lake Publishing Group
Ann Arbor, Michigan
www.cherrylakepublishing.com

Reading Adviser: Beth Walker Gambro, MS, Ed., Reading Consultant, Yorkville, IL
Content Adviser: Kelisa Wing
Book Design and Cover Art: Felicia Macheske

Photo Credits: National Archives/U.S. House of Representatives. Committee on the Judiciary. 6/3/1813-(Most Recent), Red Record of Lynching Map, National Archives Identifier: 157688056, 5; © Everett Collection/Shutterstock, 7; Library of Congress/Photographer unknown, LOC Control No.: 2006679234, 8; © mccool / Alamy Stock Photo, 11, 12; Library of Congress/Photographer unknown, LOC Control No.: 2020638851, 15; © Svineyard/Shutterstock, 17; Smithsonian Institution, National Museum of African American History and Culture Collection, Public Domain, Object No.: 2011.60.5, 17; Library of Congress/Photo Clarence Jack, LOC Control No.: 2013646995, 18; National Archives/American Red Cross, From: Tulsa Race Riot Album, National Archives Identifier: 157688056, 20; Library of Congress/Photo by American Red Cross, LOC Control No.: 2017679768, 23; Library of Congress/Photo by American Red Cross, LOC Control No.: 2017679775, 24; Library of Congress/Photo by Alvin C. Krupnick Co., LOC Control No.: 95519929, 27; Library of Congress/Photo by Alvin C. Krupnick Co., LOC Control No.: 95517748, 27; National Archives/American Red Cross, From: DR-6.08 Oklahoma, Tulsa Co. Riot Reports and Statistics, National Archives Identifier: 157670060, 28; © Alonzo J. Adams/Shutterstock, 29

Graphics Throughout: © debra hughes/Shutterstock.com; © Natewimon Nantiwat/Shutterstock.com

Cherry Lake Press is an imprint of Cherry Lake Publishing Group.

Library of Congress Cataloging-in-Publication Data
Names: Winn, Kevin P., author. | Wing, Kelisa, author.
Title: Tulsa Race Riots and the Red Summer of 1919 / written by Kevin P. Winn, Kelisa Wing.
Description: Ann Arbor, Michigan : Cherry Lake Publishing, [2022] | Series: Racial justice in America: histories | Includes index. | Audience: Grades 4-6 | Summary: "The Racial Justice in America: Histories series explores moments and eras in America's history that have been ignored or misrepresented in education due to racial bias. Tulsa Race Riots and the Red Summer of 1919 explores the events in a comprehensive, honest, and age-appropriate way. Developed in conjunction with educator, advocate, and author Kelisa Wing to reach children of all races and encourage them to approach our history with open eyes and minds. Books include 21st Century Skills and content, as well as activities created by Wing. Also includes a table of contents, glossary, index, author biography, sidebars, educational matter, and activities"— Provided by publisher.
Identifiers: LCCN 2021010786 (print) | LCCN 2021010787 (ebook) | ISBN 9781534187443 (hardcover) | ISBN 9781534188846 (paperback) | ISBN 9781534190245 (pdf) | ISBN 9781534191648 (ebook)
Subjects: LCSH: Tulsa Race Massacre, Tulsa, Okla., 1921—Juvenile literature. | African Americans—Violence against—Oklahoma—Tulsa—History—20th century—Juvenile literature. | Tulsa (Okla.)—Race relations—History—20th century—Juvenile literature.
Classification: LCC F704.T92 W55 2022 (print) | LCC F704.T92 (ebook) | DDC 305.8009766/86—dc23
LC record available at https://lccn.loc.gov/2021010786
LC ebook record available at https://lccn.loc.gov/2021010787

Cherry Lake Publishing Group would like to acknowledge the work of the Partnership for 21st Century Learning, a Network of Battelle for Kids. Please visit http://www.battelleforkids.org/networks/p21 for more information.

Printed in the United States of America

Kevin P. Winn is a children's book writer and researcher. He focuses on issues of racial justice and educational equity in his work. In 2020, Kevin earned his doctorate in Educational Policy and Evaluation from Arizona State University.

Kelisa Wing honorably served in the U.S. Army and has been an educator for 14 years. She is the author of *Promises and Possibilities: Dismantling the School to Prison Pipeline*, *If I Could: Lessons for Navigating an Unjust World*, and *Weeds & Seeds: How to Stay Positive in the Midst of Life's Storms*. She speaks both nationally and internationally about discipline reform, equity, and student engagement. Kelisa lives in Northern Virginia with her husband and two children.

CHAPTER 1

What Were the Red Summer of 1919 and the Tulsa Race Massacre?

During the summer of 1919, racist violence erupted around the United States in at least 25 cities. Many White people were angry with the progress Black people had made after emancipation. They believed in White supremacy and resented Black success and the movement toward equality. This is called White backlash. Throughout the country, mobs of White people attacked Black people. Many Black people were hurt or even killed. Because of the large amount of bloodshed, this period is called the Red Summer of 1919.

Although the violence of 1919 died down after the summer, it didn't completely disappear. Between May 31 and June 1, 1921, a White mob massacred the Black residents of the Greenwood District in Tulsa, Oklahoma.

About 15,000 Black people lived in this neighborhood. After 2 days of violence, 300 people had died, 35 city blocks were bombed and set on fire, and 9,000 Black people were left homeless.

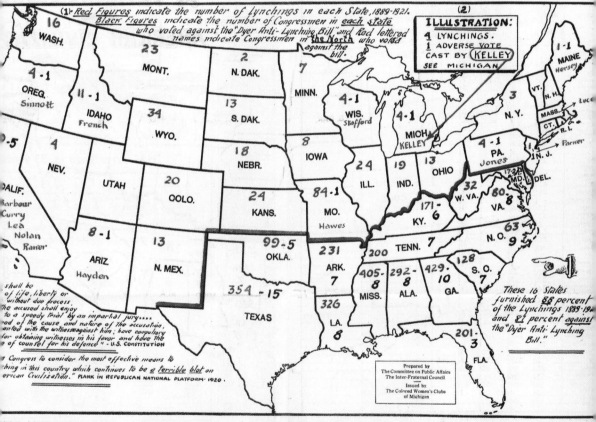

This map shows the recorded number of violent attacks against Black people in each state (red). The actual number is likely much higher.

CHAPTER 2

What Caused the Red Summer of 1919?

Many reasons were to blame for the racist riots in 1919. First, soldiers were returning home from fighting in Europe during World War I, which ended in November 1918. Some of these soldiers included Black people. They had fought for the American rights of life, liberty, and the pursuit of happiness. Black people in the United States continued to face violence from White people after slavery was outlawed in 1863. But Black soldiers believed that their military service would be appreciated when they returned home. They hoped they would be treated better. Unfortunately, the opposite happened. White people attacked and murdered Black veterans in the United States.

A regiment of Black infantrymen in WWI, nicknamed the Harlem Hellfighters.

A second reason for the Red Summer was the beginning of the Great Migration. About 1 million Black people moved north to escape violence in the South. White terrorist groups like the Ku Klux Klan (KKK) in the South terrorized Black people. The KKK worked to continue White supremacy. In order to keep control over Black people, the KKK attacked Black people throughout the South and other states as well. The KKK killed Black people in public and violent ways. These murders often took the form of racial terror lynchings. Black people moved north to escape the KKK, but they generally were not welcomed by northerners either.

The KKK had chapters and members all across the United States in the early 1900s.

Another important reason for the racist rioting was a bad economy. The United States didn't have enough jobs for everyone. During WWI, Black people who had moved north were hired for jobs that White soldiers had left to fight in WWI. When White soldiers returned home, they were angry that Black people had the jobs they previously held. Business owners listened to the White veterans' complaints and fired Black people. White veterans were rehired.

These reasons all add up to White backlash. White people resented the success and advancement of Black people and responded with violence.

Black World War I veterans who returned to the South were often lynched when wearing their army uniforms. White people who didn't want Black people to gain power saw Black veterans in army uniforms as a threat. They didn't want Black people to have basic **human rights** when they returned to the United States.

CHAPTER 3

Where Were the Racist Riots of the Red Summer of 1919?

The racist riots and massacres took place in approximately 25 cities around the United States. Most of the violence took place in the South. But racist riots occurred in the Northeast, Southwest, and Midwest too. Each of these racist riots and massacres deserves attention. However, two of the most violent ones occurred in Chicago, Illinois, and Elaine, Arkansas.

After a violent racist riot in Washington, D.C., left 40 people dead, the violence spread to Chicago on July 27, 1919. On a hot day in the city, four Black boys went into Lake Michigan on a homemade raft to cool off. The boys accidentally crossed the invisible line that unofficially divided the Black and White sections of the beach and lake. Angered by this, a White man named George Stauber threw a stone at them. He struck one of the boys, Eugene Williams, in the head. Eugene fell beneath the surface and drowned. He was only 17 years old.

Racist riots happen when one race takes up arms and inflicts violence against another race.

The riot in Chicago lasted a whole week.

When a White police officer refused to arrest George Stauber for murder, Black people protested. In response, White mobs formed and attacked Black neighborhoods. They shot Black people with guns and burned down their homes. After a week of violence, 38 people were dead, 23 of whom were Black. Another 1,000 families were homeless.

Just outside of Elaine, Arkansas, a group of Black sharecroppers met to discuss how they could be paid fairly by White landowners. White people, angry that Black people wanted better treatment, attacked the meeting. When a White police officer was shot and killed, the White mob murdered all Black people in sight. Even the governor of Arkansas ordered 500 soldiers to kill Black people in Elaine. Historians think that by the end of the massacre, White people had murdered more than 200 Black people. The exact number murdered remains a mystery. White people dumped bodies into the river to hide evidence of their crimes. After the violence, no White people were arrested, but 12 Black men were charged with murder.

U.S. soldiers were ordered to kill Black Americans in Elaine, Arkansas.

CHAPTER 4

The Tulsa Race Massacre

In 1906, a Black man named O. W. Gurley established the Greenwood District in Tulsa, Oklahoma. Because of the segregation laws in the state, only Black people lived in Greenwood. Tulsa was growing fast at this time because of the discovery of oil, which attracted White and Black people. As more Black people moved to Tulsa, the Greenwood District became one of the wealthiest areas in the United States. Many successful small businesses, the largest Black-owned hotel in the country, and three millionaires were located in the Greenwood District. Because of this wealth, the Greenwood District became known as Black Wall Street.

While Greenwood was destroyed during the massacre, today the area looks a bit like it did before 1921.

Two years after the Red Summer of 1919, Black Wall Street became the site of one of the deadliest events in U.S. history: the Tulsa Race Massacre. During the 2-day massacre, White mobs destroyed Black Wall Street.

Similar to the Red Summer 2 years earlier, racist White people were angry at and jealous of successful Black people. They looked for an excuse to act upon their rage. They found their excuse on May 31, 1921. A 19-year-old Black shoe shiner named Dick Rowland was accused of hurting a White woman named Sarah Page. Page eventually denied that Rowland had harmed her. But it was too late. Newspapers learned of the false story and published it.

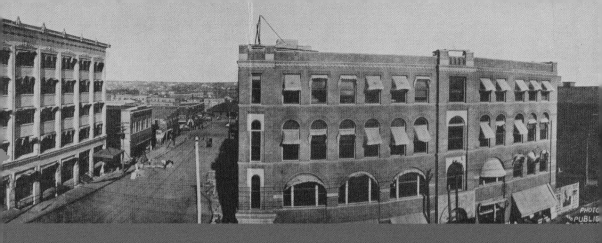

On May 31, 1921, Rowland was arrested and put in jail. A White mob formed outside of the jail. Worried that Rowland would be lynched, Black people from the Greenwood District went to defend the jail. A scuffle broke out, and White people began the violence that destroyed Black Wall Street.

During this time in U.S. history, newspapers owned by White people often published stories that lied about Black people. White writers blamed Black people for crimes they hadn't committed. Before finding out the truth, White mobs formed. These mobs punished Black people, lynching and murdering them.

The Greenwood neighborhood in Tulsa was reduced to rubble.

A crowd of more than 1,000 White people descended upon Black Wall Street. The White mob murdered Black people who stood in their way. White men, women, and children as young as 10 participated in the violence. White people looted Black-owned homes and set them on fire. By the end of the massacre, the White mob had murdered 300 Black people. They set fire to and air-bombed 35 city blocks. By the end of the day on June 1, 10,000 Black people were left homeless.

Nobody in the Black community was safe from the racist violence. Even Black people who had formed positive relationships with White Tulsans were murdered. Dr. Arthur C. Jackson, one of the most famous Black doctors in the country, served both Black and White people. A White teenager shot him to death.

CHAPTER 5

Aftermath of the Tulsa Race Massacre

Black Tulsans faced internment in tents after the massacre. Even though they hadn't started the violence, White people treated them like criminals. For days, Black people were forced into one of two areas of the city where they were held captive. They couldn't leave unless a White person gave them permission.

Immediately after the massacre, a White newspaper in town published an article claiming that this incident should never happen again. But the author wasn't referring to the massacre. He meant that Black people should never be allowed to rebuild another neighborhood like Black Wall Street. Soon, White business owners tried to force Black people out of Tulsa. They offered to buy land from Black people for very low and unfair prices. In fact, the city even tried to pass laws that would have made it impossible for Black people to rebuild on their own land.

Black Tulsans were prisoners in the city following the massacre.

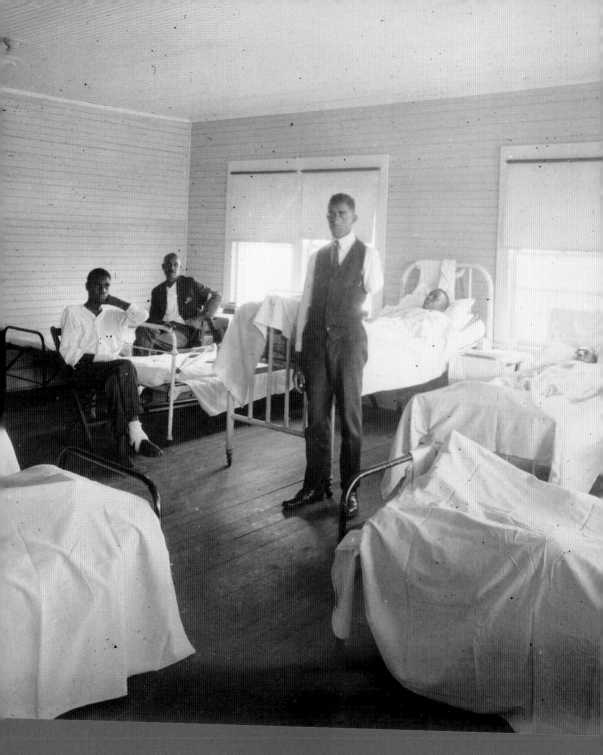

Before the Tulsa Massacre, the Red Cross usually only served American armed forces or assisted after events like earthquakes or tornadoes.

Disgusted by White Tulsans' behavior, the American Red Cross helped Black Tulsans. This was the first time the Red Cross had helped in an event like this. The Red Cross sheltered homeless Black Tulsans who had lost everything in the massacre.

After the massacre, many Black people refused to let White Tulsans bully them. They refused to be chased out of town. Instead, Black people worked harder than ever to rebuild what they had lost. White leaders in Tulsa continued making life difficult. They didn't allow Black people to get the money they deserved. Black business owners who lost their buildings in the fires received no money to replace their property. Instead, they were blamed for the massacre.

CHAPTER 6

Hidden History: No Justice for Massacre Victims

The Red Summer of 1919 and the Tulsa Race Massacre aren't part of many history textbooks. The events and people who experienced them aren't widely known. There are some important reasons for this. People in power at the time—usually White people—worked to keep these events a secret. Another reason is that the memories of these events were too painful for survivors to talk about. And sometimes, survivors who wanted to talk couldn't trust the people in power with their stories.

White people who murdered and injured hundreds of Black people almost always got away with their crimes. No White people received a legal conviction for participating in the Tulsa Race Massacre.

During the Tulsa Massacre, Black people were rounded up and removed from their homes and neighborhood.

In these riots, White people got away with murdering Black people. White people believed Black people were dangerous criminals. But it was White individuals, mobs, and police who tortured and killed their fellow humans. They looted and destroyed Black-owned property. To this day, victims of these crimes haven't received justice. Families of Black people who were falsely accused of starting riots and massacres have tried to find justice. For many years, families have worked to make sure their relatives are no longer blamed.

J. B. Stradford ran the largest Black-owned hotel in the United States. He was falsely accused of starting the Tulsa Race Massacre. His family fought to clear his name even after he died. Because of his family's hard work, the state of Oklahoma declared J. B. Stradford innocent in 1996.

ROUNDUP OF 64 INDICTED BLACKS IS ON

No Warrants Issued for Whites

Today, people advocate for racial justice in Tulsa.

Thankfully, there were brave writers like Mary E. Jones Parrish. As a Black woman, she risked anger from White people by publishing a book called *Race Riot 1921: Events of the Tulsa Disaster*. Because of her, we have details about what occurred during the Tulsa Race Massacre. However, not many original copies of this book exist. Some historians believe that White leaders in Tulsa bought many copies of the book to hide the truth. Even though the massacre made national news, Tulsa's leaders were embarrassed by the bad publicity. They weren't embarrassed by the way they treated Black people, though. Rather than helping to rebuild Black Wall Street, White people worked to keep the details of the massacre hidden.

The Red Summer of 1919 and the Tulsa Race Massacre of 1921 are important parts of American history. They show how racist violence against Black people is often ignored. They also reveal how White people with power work to keep this racism a secret. By uncovering the truth, we can work to prevent these events from happening again.

SHOW WHAT YOU KNOW

Do you know that the truth matters? Throughout history, many innocent people and communities have suffered because someone decided to tell a lie. For example, a massacre occurred in Rosewood, Florida, in 1922. A White woman named Fannie Taylor lied about being attacked by a Black man. As a result of her lie, the entire town of Rosewood was destroyed and burned to the ground. No one was arrested. In 1994, Arnett Doctor and other child survivors of the attack sued the state of Florida. They won and received an apology from the governor for what happened.

For this project, research another time in history or in the present where a lie damaged a community or person. Share why you think the truth is important and how you can encourage others to be truthful.

Do you know there are so many different ways to show what you know? Rather than using traditional ways to display knowledge, try something new to complete this assignment. Here are some ideas:

1. Rap
2. Mural
3. Musical
4. Debate
5. Web page
6. Speech
7. Bulletin board
8. Jigsaw puzzle
9. Show and tell
10. Essay
11. Diorama
12. Performance
13. Podcast
14. Journal
15. OR add your own...

EXTEND YOUR LEARNING

Ellis Tucci. "Red Summer," in *Hidden History*, podcast, June 27, 2020, https://www.hiddenhistory.show/episodes-1/red-summer. Accessed February 1, 2021.

Nia Clark. *Dreams of Black Wall Street*, podcast, January 20, 2020, https://www.dreamsofblackwallstreet.com. Accessed February 1, 2021.

Ursula Wolfe-Rocca. "The Red Summer of 1919, Explained," **Teen Vogue**, May 31, 2020, https://www.teenvogue.com/story/the-red-summer-of-1919-explained. Accessed December 17, 2020.

GLOSSARY

captive (KAP-tiv) held against one's will

emancipation (ih-man-suh-PAY-shuhn) freedom from something

Great Migration (GRAYT mye-GRAY-shuhn) the period between 1916 and 1970 when 6 million Black people moved from the South to other parts of the United States

human rights (HYOO-muhn RITES) rights that should belong to each individual person

internment (in-TURN-muhnt) being held against your will, often during wars

legal conviction (LEE-guhl kuhn-VIK-shuhn) finding a person to be guilty of a crime

massacred (MAH-suh-kur) brutally killed a large number of people

racial terror lynchings (RAY-shuhl TER-uhr LINCH-ings) violent attacks by White people on BIPOC, especially Black people, to scare and control them; usually done through torture, murder, and hanging

racist riots (RAY-sist RYE-uhts) violence against BIPOC by a group of people with the intent to harm them or their livelihoods

segregation (seg-ruh-GAY-shuhn) keeping people or groups apart

sharecroppers (SHER-krah-puhrs) people who rent a plot of land from the owner to farm their own crops

White backlash (WITE BAK-lash) the negative, and sometimes violent, response some White people have to the progress of other racial or ethnic groups

White supremacy (WITE suh-PREH-muh-see) the incorrect belief that White people and their ideas are superior to all others

INDEX